George Mikes was born in 1912 in Siklos, Hungary. He studied law and received his doctorate at Budapest University. At the same time he became a journalist and was sent to London as a correspondent to cover the Munich crisis. He came for a fortnight and has stayed ever since. During the war he was engaged in broadcasting to Hungary and at the time of the Revolution he went back to cover that event for B.B.C. television.

Mr Mikes now works as a critic, broadcaster and writer. His books include: *The Hungarian Revolution, Über Alles, Little Cabbages, Shakespeare and Myself, Italy for Beginners, How to Unite Nations; How to be an Alien, How to be Inimitable, How to Scrape Skies* and *How to Tango* he wrote in collaboration with Nicolas Bentley, and he has also published a novel, *Mortal Passion*. Several of these are published in Penguins. His latest publications are *George Mikes Introduces Switzerland* (1977; edited by Raffael Ganz), *How to be Decadent* (1977; Nicolas Bentley drew the pictures) and *Tsi-Tsa* (1978).

Mr Mikes is married with two children and enjoys getting away from the countryside.

Nicolas Bentley was born in Highgate in 1907 and educated at University College School, London and Heatherley School of Art. He was an artist, author, publisher and illustrator of more than sixty books – including works by Belloc, T. S. Eliot, Damon Runyon, Lawrence Durrell and many others. He died in 1978.

It's easy

GEORGE MIKES

How to be an Alien

A HANDBOOK FOR BEGINNERS AND
ADVANCED PUPILS

Nicolas Bentley drew the pictures

PENGUIN BOOKS

Penguin Books Ltd, Harmondsworth, Middlesex, England
Penguin Books, 625 Madison Avenue, New York, New York 10022, U.S.A.
Penguin Books Australia Ltd, Ringwood, Victoria, Australia
Penguin Books Canada Ltd, 2801 John Street, Markham, Ontario, Canada L3R 1B4
Penguin Books (N.Z.) Ltd, 182–190 Wairau Road, Auckland 10, New Zealand

—

First published by André Deutsch 1946
Published in Penguin Books 1966
Reprinted 1968, 1969, 1970, 1971, 1972, 1973, 1974, 1975, 1976, 1977, 1978 (twice),
1979, 1980, 1981

—

Copyright 1946 © by George Mikes and Nicolas Bentley
All rights reserved

—

Made and printed in Great Britain by
Hazell Watson & Viney Ltd,
Aylesbury, Bucks
Set in Linotype Baskerville

Except in the United States of America,
this book is sold subject to the condition
that it shall not, by way of trade or otherwise,
be lent, re-sold, hired out, or otherwise circulated
without the publisher's prior consent in any form of
binding or cover other than that in which it is
published and without a similar condition
including this condition being imposed
on the subsequent purchaser

CONTENTS

'I have seen much to hate here, much to forgive. But in a world where England is finished and dead, I do not wish to live.'

ALICE DUER MILLER: *The White Cliffs*

PREFACE TO THE 24th IMPRESSION

THE reception given to this book when it first appeared in the autumn of 1946, was at once a pleasant surprise and a disappointment for me. A surprise, because the reception was so kind; a disappointment for the same reason.

Let me explain.

The first part of this statement needs little amplification. Even people who are not closely connected with the publishing trade will be able to realize that it is very nice – I'm sorry, I'd better be a little more English: a not totally unpleasant thing for a completely unknown author to run into three impressions within a few weeks of publication and thereafter into another twenty-one.

What is my grievance, then? It is that this book has completely changed the picture I used to cherish of myself. This was to be a book of defiance. Before its publication I felt myself a man who was going to tell the English where to get off. I had spoken my mind regardless of consequences; I thought I was brave and outspoken and expected either to go unnoticed or to face a storm. But no storm came. I expected the English to be up in arms against me but they patted me on the back; I expected the British nation to rise in wrath but all they said, was: 'quite amusing'. It was indeed a bitter disappointment.

While the Rumanian Radio was serializing (without my permission) *How to be an Alien* as an anti-British tract, the Central Office of Information rang me up here in London and asked me to allow the book to be translated into Polish for the benefit of those many

Polish refugees who were then settling in this country. 'We want our friends to see us in this light,' the man said on the telephone. This was hard to bear for my militant and defiant spirit. 'But it's not such a favourable light,' I protested feebly. 'It's a very human light and that is the most favourable,' retorted the official. I was crushed.

A few weeks later my drooping spirit was revived when I heard of a suburban bank manager whose wife had brought this book home to him remarking that she had found it fairly amusing. The gentleman in question sat down in front of his open fire, put his feet up and read the book right through with a continually darkening face. When he had finished, he stood up and said :

'Downright impertinence.'

And threw the book into the fire.

He was a noble and patriotic spirit and he did me a great deal of good. I wished there had been more like him in England. But I could never find another.

Since then I have actually written about a dozen books; but I might as well have never written anything else. I remained the author of *How to be an Alien* even after I had published a collection of serious essays. Even Mr Somerset Maugham complained about this type of treatment bitterly and repeatedly. Whatever he did, he was told that he would never write another *Of Human Bondage*; Arnold Bennett in spite of fifty other works remained the author of *The Old Wives' Tale* and nothing else; and Mr Robert Graves is just the author of the Claudius books. These authors are much more eminent than I am; but their problem is the same. At the moment I am engaged in writing a 750-page picaresque novel set in ancient Sumeria. It is taking shape nicely and I am going to get the Nobel Prize for it. But it will be of no use: I shall still remain the author of *How to be an Alien*.

I am not complaining. One's books start living their independent lives soon enough, just like one's children. I love this book; it has done almost as much for me as I have done for it. Yet, however loving a parent you may be, it hurts your pride a little if you are only known, acknowledged and accepted as the father of your eldest child.

In 1946 I took this manuscript to André Deutsch, a young man who had just decided to try his luck as a publisher. He used to go, once upon a time, to the same school as my younger brother. I knew him from the old days and it was quite obvious to me even then, in Budapest, when he was only twelve and wore shorts, that he would make an excellent publisher in London if he only had the chance. So I offered my book to him and as, at that time, he could not get manuscripts from better known authors, he accepted it with a sigh. He suggested that Nicolas Bentley should be asked to 'draw the pictures'. I liked the idea but I said he would turn the suggestion down. Once again I was right: he did turn it down. Eventually, however, he was persuaded to change his mind.

Mr Deutsch was at that time working for a different firm. Four years after the publication of this book, and after the subsequent publication of three other Mikes-Bentley books, he left this firm while I stayed with them and went on working with another popular and able cartoonist, David Langdon. Now, however, André Deutsch has bought all the rights of my past and future output from his former firm and the original team of Deutsch, Bentley and myself are together again under the imprint of the first named gentleman. We are all twelve years older and Mr Deutsch does not wear shorts any more, or not in the office, at any rate.

'When are you going to write another *How to be an Alien*?' Deutsch and Bentley ask me from time to time and I am sure they mean it kindly.

They cannot quite make out the reply I mutter in answer to their friendly query. It is:

'Never, if I can help it.'

London, May 1958   GEORGE MIKES

PREFACE

I BELIEVE, without undue modesty, that I have certain qualifications to write on 'how to be an alien.' I am an alien myself. What is more, I have been an alien all my life. Only during the first twenty-six years of my life I was not aware of this plain fact. I was living in my own country, a country full of aliens, and I noticed nothing particular or irregular about myself; then I came to England, and you can imagine my painful surprise.

Like all great and important discoveries it was a matter of a few seconds. You probably all know from your schooldays how Isaac Newton discovered the law of gravitation. An apple fell on his head. This incident set him thinking for a minute or two, then he exclaimed joyfully: 'Of course! The gravitation constant is the acceleration per second that a mass of one gram causes at a distance of one centimetre.' You were also taught that James Watt one day went into the kitchen where cabbage was cooking and saw the lid of the saucepan rise and fall. 'Now let me think,' he murmured – 'let me think.' Then he struck his forehead and the steam engine was discovered. It was the same with me, although circumstances were rather different.

It was like this. Some years ago I spent a lot of time with a young lady who was very proud and conscious of being English. Once she asked me – to my great surprise – whether I would marry her. 'No,' I replied, 'I will not. My mother would never agree to my marrying a foreigner.' She looked at me a little surprised and irritated, and retorted: 'I, a foreigner? What a silly thing to say. I am English. You are the foreigner. And your mother, too.' I did not give in. 'In Budapest, too?' I asked her. 'Everywhere,' she declared with determination. 'Truth does not depend on geography. What is true in England is also true in Hungary and in North Borneo and Venezuela and everywhere.'

I saw that this theory was as irrefutable as it was simple. I was startled and upset. Mainly because of my mother whom I loved and respected. Now, I suddenly learned what she really was.

It was a shame and bad taste to be an alien, and it is no use pretending otherwise. There is no way out of it. A criminal may improve and become a decent member of society. A foreigner cannot improve. Once a foreigner, always a foreigner. There is no way out for him. He may become British; he can never become English.

So it is better to reconcile yourself to the sorrowful reality. There are some noble English people who might forgive you. There are some magnanimous souls who realize that it is not your fault, only your misfortune. They will treat you with condescension, understanding and sympathy. They will invite you to their homes. Just as they keep lap-dogs and other pets, they are quite prepared to keep a few foreigners.

The title of this book, *How to be an Alien*, consequently expresses more than it should. How to be an alien? One should not be an alien at all. There are certain rules, however, which have to be followed if you want to make yourself as acceptable and civilized as you possibly can.

Study these rules, and imitate the English. There can be only one result: if you don't succeed in imitating them you become ridiculous; if you do, you become even more ridiculous.

G. M.

I. How to be a General Alien

A WARNING TO BEGINNERS

IN ENGLAND * everything is the other way round.

On Sundays on the Continent even the poorest person puts on his best suit, tries to look respectable, and at the same time the life of the country becomes gay and cheerful; in England even the richest peer or motor-manufacturer dresses in some peculiar rags, does not shave, and the country becomes dull and dreary. On the Continent there is one topic which should be avoided — the weather; in England, if you do not repeat the phrase 'Lovely day, isn't it?' at least two hundred times a day, you are considered a bit dull. On the Continent Sunday papers appear on Monday; in England — a country of exotic oddities — they appear on Sunday. On the Continent people use a fork as though a fork were a shovel; in England they turn it upside down and push everything — including peas — on top of it.

On a continental bus approaching a request-stop the conductor rings the bell if he wants his bus to go on without stopping; in England you ring the bell if you want the bus to stop. On the Continent stray cats are judged individually on their merit — some are loved, some are only respected; in England they are universally worshipped as in ancient Egypt. On the Continent

---

* When people say England, they sometimes mean Great Britain, sometimes the United Kingdom, sometimes the British Isles — but never England.

Sabbath morn

people have good food; in England people have good table manners.

On the Continent public orators try to learn to speak fluently and smoothly; in England they take a special course in Oxonian stuttering. On the Continent learned persons love to quote Aristotle, Horace, Montaigne and show off their knowledge; in England only uneducated people show off their knowledge, nobody quotes Latin and Greek authors in the course of a conversation, unless he has never read them.

On the Continent almost every nation whether little or great has openly declared at one time or another that it is superior to all other nations; the English fight heroic wars to combat these dangerous ideas without ever mentioning which is *really* the most superior race in the world. Continental people are sensitive and touchy; the English take everything with an exquisite sense of humour – they are only offended if you tell them that they have no sense of humour. On the Continent the population consists of a small percentage of criminals, a small percentage of honest people and the rest are a vague transition between the two; in England you find a small percentage of criminals and the rest are honest people. On the other hand, people on the Continent either tell you the truth or lie; in England they hardly ever lie, but they would not dream of telling you the truth.

Many continentals think life is a game; the English think cricket is a game.

INTRODUCTION

THIS is a chapter on how to introduce people to one another.

The aim of introduction is to conceal a person's identity. It is very important that you should not pronounce anybody's name in a way that the other party may be able to catch it. Generally speaking, your pronunciation is a sound guarantee for that. On the other hand, if you are introduced to someone there are two important rules to follow.

1. If he stretches out his hand in order to shake yours, you must not accept it. Smile vaguely, and as soon as he gives up the hope of shaking you by the hand, you stretch out your own hand and try to catch *his* in vain. This game is repeated until the greater part of the afternoon or evening has elapsed. It is extremely likely that this will be the most amusing part of the afternoon or evening, anyway.

2. Once the introduction has been made you have to inquire after the health of your new acquaintance.

Try the thing in your own language. Introduce the persons, let us say, in French and murmur their names. Should they shake hands and ask:

'Comment allez-vous?'

'Comment allez-vous?' – it will be a capital joke, remembered till their last days.

Do not forget, however, that your new friend who makes this touchingly kind inquiry after your state of health does not care in the least whether you are well and kicking or dying of delirium tremens. A dialogue like this:

HE: 'How d'you do?'

YOU: 'General state of health fairly satisfactory. Slight insomnia and a rather bad corn on left foot. Blood pressure low, digestion slow but normal.'

– well, such a dialogue would be unforgivable.

In the next phase you must not say 'Pleased to meet you.' This is one of the very few lies you must never utter because, for some unknown reason, it is considered vulgar. You must not say 'Pleased to meet you,' even if you are definitely disgusted with the man.

A few general remarks:

1. Do not click your heels, do not bow, leave off gymnastic and choreographic exercises altogether for the moment.

2. Do not call foreign lawyers, teachers, dentists, commercial travellers and estate agents 'Doctor.' Everybody knows that the little word 'doctor' only means that they are Central Europeans. This is painful enough in itself, you do not need to remind people of it all the time.

Which hand will you have?

THE WEATHER

THIS is the most important topic in the land. Do not be misled by memories of your youth when, on the Continent, wanting to describe someone as exceptionally dull, you remarked: 'He is the type who would discuss the weather with you.' In England this is an ever-interesting, even thrilling topic, and you must be good at discussing the weather.

EXAMPLES FOR CONVERSATION
For Good Weather

'Lovely day, isn't it?'
'Isn't it *beautiful*?'
'The sun . . .'
'Isn't it gorgeous?'
'Wonderful, isn't it?'
'It's so nice and hot . . .'
'Personally, I think it's so nice when it's hot— isn't it?'
'I adore it – don't you?'

For Bad Weather

'Nasty day, isn't it?'
'Isn't it dreadful?'
'The rain . . . I hate rain . . .'
'I don't like it at all. Do you?'
'Fancy such a day in July. Rain in the morning, then a bit of sunshine, and then rain, rain, rain, all day long.'
'I remember exactly the same July day in 1936.'
'Yes, I remember too.'
'Or was it in 1928?'
'Yes, it was.'

'*Good afternoon!*'

'Or in 1939?'
'Yes, that's right.'

Now observe the last few sentences of this conversation. A very important rule emerges from it. You must
never contradict anybody when discussing the weather.
Should it hail and snow, should hurricanes uproot the
trees from the sides of the road, and should someone
remark to you: 'Nice day, isn't it?' – answer without
hesitation: 'Isn't it lovely?'

Learn the above conversation by heart. If you are a
bit slow in picking things up, learn at least one conversation, it would do wonderfully for any occasion.

If you do not say anything else for the rest of your
life, just repeat this conversation, you still have a fair
chance of passing as a remarkably witty man of sharp
intellect, keen observation and extremely pleasant
manners.

English society is a class society, strictly organized
almost on corporative lines. If you doubt this, listen to
the weather forecasts. There is always a different
weather forecast for farmers. You often hear statements
like this on the radio:

'To-morrow it will be cold, cloudy and foggy; long
periods of rain will be interrupted by short periods of
showers.'

And then:

'Weather forecast for farmers. It will be fair and
warm, many hours of sunshine.'

You must not forget that the farmers do grand work
of national importance and deserve better weather.

It happened on innumerable occasions that nice,
warm weather had been forecast and rain and snow
fell all day long, or *vice versa*. Some people jumped

rashly to the conclusion that something must be wrong with the weather forecasts. They are mistaken and should be more careful with their allegations.

I have read an article in one of the Sunday papers and now I can tell you what the situation really is. All troubles are caused by anti-cyclones. (I don't quite know what anti-cyclones are, but this is not important; I hate cyclones and am very anti-cyclone myself.) The two naughtiest anti-cyclones are the Azores and the Polar anti-cyclones.

The British meteorologists forecast the *right* weather – as it really *should* be – and then these impertinent little anti-cyclones interfere and mess up everything.

That again proves that if the British kept to themselves and did not mix with foreign things like Polar and Azores anti-cyclones they would be much better off.

SOUL AND UNDERSTATEMENT

FOREIGNERS have souls; the English haven't.

On the Continent you find any amount of people who sigh deeply for no conspicuous reason, yearn, suffer and look in the air extremely sadly. This is soul.

The worst kind of soul is the great Slav soul. People who suffer from it are usually very deep thinkers. They may say things like this: 'Sometimes I am so merry and sometimes I am so sad. Can you explain why?' (You cannot, do not try.) Or they may say: 'I am so mysterious. . . . I sometimes wish I were somewhere else than where I am.' (Do not say: 'I wish you were.') Or 'When I am alone in a forest at night-time and jump from one tree to another, I often think that life is so strange.'

All this is very deep: and just soul, nothing else.

The English have no soul; they have the understatement instead.

If a continental youth wants to declare his love to a girl, he kneels down, tells her that she is the sweetest, the most charming and ravishing person in the world, that she has *something* in her, something peculiar and individual which only a few hundred thousand other women have and that he would be unable to live one more minute without her. Often, to give a little more emphasis to the statement, he shoots himself on the spot. This is a normal, week-day declaration of love in the more temperamental continental countries. In England the boy pats his adored one on the back and says softly: 'I don't object to you, you know.' If he is quite mad with passion, he may add: 'I rather fancy you, in fact.'

If he wants to marry a girl, he says:

'*My soul is all an Aching Void*' – John Wesley

'I say ... would you? ...'
If he wants to make an indecent proposal:
'I say ... what about ...'

   Overstatement, too, plays a considerable part in English social life. This takes mostly the form of someone remarking: 'I say ...' and then keeping silent for three days on end.

TEA

THE trouble with tea is that originally it was quite a good drink.

So a group of the most eminent British scientists put their heads together, and made complicated biological experiments to find a way of spoiling it.

To the eternal glory of British science their labour bore fruit. They suggested that if you do not drink it clear, or with lemon or rum and sugar, but pour a few drops of cold milk into it, and no sugar at all, the desired object is achieved. Once this refreshing, aromatic, oriental beverage was successfully transformed into colourless and tasteless gargling-water, it suddenly became the national drink of Great Britain and Ireland – still retaining, indeed usurping, the high-sounding title of tea.

There are some occasions when you must not refuse a cup of tea, otherwise you are judged an exotic and barbarous bird without any hope of ever being able to take your place in civilised society.

If you are invited to an English home, at five o'clock in the morning you get a cup of tea. It is either brought in by a heartily smiling hostess or an almost malevolently silent maid. When you are disturbed in your sweetest morning sleep you must not say: 'Madame (or Mabel), I think you are a cruel, spiteful and malignant person who deserves to be shot.' On the contrary, you have to declare with your best five o'clock smile: 'Thank you so much. I do adore a cup of early morning tea, especially early in the morning.' If they leave you alone with the liquid, you may pour it down the washbasin.

Then you have tea for breakfast; then you have tea at eleven o'clock in the morning; then after lunch;

The cup that cheers

then you have tea for tea; then after supper; and again at eleven o'clock at night.

You must not refuse any additional cups of tea under the following circumstances: if it is hot; if it is cold; if you are tired; if anybody thinks that you might be tired; if you are nervous; if you are gay; before you go out; if you are out; if you have just returned home; if you feel like it; if you do not feel like it; if you have had no tea for some time; if you have just had a cup.

You definitely must not follow my example. I sleep at five o'clock in the morning; I have coffee for breakfast; I drink innumerable cups of black coffee during the day; I have the most unorthodox and exotic teas even at tea-time.

The other day, for instance – I just mention this as a terrifying example to show you how low some people can sink – I wanted a cup of coffee and a piece of cheese for tea. It was one of those exceptionally hot days and my wife (once a good Englishwoman, now completely and hopelessly led astray by my wicked foreign influence) made some cold coffee and put it in the refrigerator, where it froze and became one solid block. On the other hand, she left the cheese on the kitchen table, where it melted. So I had a piece of coffee and a glass of cheese.

SEX

CONTINENTAL people have sex life; the English have hot-water bottles.

A WORD ON SOME PUBLISHERS

I HEARD of a distinguished, pure-minded English publisher who adapted John Steinbeck's novel, *The Grapes of Wrath*, so skilfully that it became a charming little family book on grapes and other fruits, with many illustrations.

On the other hand, a continental publisher in London had a French political book, *The Popular Front*, translated into English. It became an exciting, pornographic book, called *The Popular Behind*.

THE LANGUAGE

WHEN I arrived in England I thought I knew English. After I'd been here an hour I realized that I did not understand one word. In the first week I picked up a tolerable working knowledge of the language and the the next seven years convinced me gradually but thoroughly that I would never know it really well, let alone perfectly. This is sad. My only consolation being that nobody speaks English perfectly.

Remember that those five hundred words an average Englishman uses are far from being the whole vocabulary of the language. You may learn another five hundred and another five thousand and yet another fifty thousand and still you may come across a further fifty thousand you have never heard of before, and nobody else either.

If you live here long enough you will find out to your greatest amazement that the adjective *nice* is not the only adjective the language possesses, in spite of the fact that in the first three years you do not need to learn or use any other adjectives. You can say that the weather is nice, a restaurant is nice, Mr Soandso is nice, Mrs Soandso's clothes are nice, you had a nice time, and all this will be very nice.

Then you have to decide on your accent. You will have your foreign accent all right, but many people like to mix it with something else. I knew a Polish Jew who had a strong Yiddish-Irish accent. People found it fascinating though slightly exaggerated. The easiest way to give the impression of having a good accent or no foreign accent at all is to hold an unlit pipe in your mouth, to mutter between your teeth and finish all your sentences with the question: 'isn't it?' People will not understand much, but they are accustomed to that and they will get a most excellent impression.

I have known quite a number of foreigners who tried hard to acquire an Oxford accent. The advantage of this is that you give the idea of being permanently in the company of Oxford dons and lecturers on medieval numismatics; the disadvantage is that the permanent singing is rather a strain on your throat and that it is a type of affection that even many English people find it hard to keep up incessantly. You may fall out of it, speak naturally, and then where are you?

The Mayfair accent can be highly recommended, too. The advantages of Mayfair English are that it unites the affected air of the Oxford accent with the uncultured flavour of a half-educated professional hotel-dancer.

The most successful attempts, however, to put on a highly cultured air have been made on the polysyllabic lines. Many foreigners who have learnt Latin and Greek in school discover with amazement and satisfaction that the English language has absorbed a huge amount of ancient Latin and Greek expressions, and they realize that (*a*) it is much easier to learn these expressions than the much simpler English words; (*b*) that these words as a rule are interminably long and make a simply superb impression when talking to the greengrocer, the porter and the insurance agent.

Imagine, for instance, that the porter of the block of flats where you live remarks sharply that you must not put your dustbin out in front of your door before 7.30 a.m. Should you answer 'Please don't bully me,' a loud and tiresome argument may follow, and certainly the porter will be proved right, because you are sure to find a clause in your contract (small print, bottom

The pipe trick

of last page) that the porter is always right and you owe absolute allegiance and unconditional obedience to him. Should you answer, however, with these words: 'I repudiate your petulant expostulations,' the argument will be closed at once, the porter will be proud of having such a highly cultured man in the block, and from that day onwards you may, if you please, get up at four o'clock in the morning and hang your dustbin out of the window.

But even in Curzon Street society, if you say, for instance, that you are a *tough guy* they will consider you a vulgar, irritating and objectionable person. Should you declare, however, that you are *an inquisitorial and peremptory homo sapiens,* they will have no idea what you mean, but they will feel in their bones that you must be something wonderful.

When you know all the long words it is advisable to start learning some of the short ones, too.

You should be careful when using these endless words. An acquaintance of mine once was fortunate enough to discover the most impressive word *notalgia* for back-ache. Mistakenly, however, he declared in a large company:

'I have such a nostalgia.'

'Oh, you want to go home to Nizhne-Novgorod?' asked his most sympathetic hostess.

'Not at all,' he answered. 'I just cannot sit down.'

Finally, there are two important points to remember:

1. Do not forget that it is much easier to write in English than to speak English, because you can *write* without a foreign accent.

2. In a bus and in other public places it is more advisable to speak softly in good German than to shout in abominable English.

Anyway, this whole language business is not at all easy. After spending eight years in this country, the other day I was told by a very kind lady: 'But why do you complain? You really speak a most excellent accent without the slightest English.'

HOW NOT TO BE CLEVER

'You foreigners are so clever,' said a lady to me some years ago. First, thinking of the great amount of foreign idiots and half-wits I had had the honour of meeting, I considered this remark exaggerated but complimentary.

Since then I have learnt that it was far from it. These few words expressed the lady's contempt and slight disgust for foreigners.

If you look up the word *clever* in any English dictionary, you will find that the dictionaries are out of date and mislead you on this point. According to the Pocket Oxford Dictionary, for instance, the word means quick and neat in movement . . . skilful, talented, ingenious. Nuttall's Dictionary gives these meanings: dexterous, skilful, ingenious, quick or ready-witted, intelligent. All nice adjectives, expressing valuable and estimable characteristics. A modern Englishman, however, uses the word *clever* in the sense: shrewd, sly, furtive, surreptitious, treacherous, sneaking, crafty, un-English, un-Scottish, un-Welsh.

In England it is bad manners to be clever, to assert something confidently. It may be your own personal view that two and two make four, but you must not state it in a self-assured way, because this is a democratic country and others may be of a different opinion.

A continental gentleman seeing a nice panorama may remark:

'This view rather reminds me of Utrecht, where the peace treaty concluding the War of Spanish Succession was signed on the 11th April, 1713. The river there, however, recalls the Guadalquivir, which rises in the

'*Dr Hoffmeyer is absolutely* brilliant'

Sierra de Cazorla and flows south-west to the Atlantic Ocean and is 650 kilometres long. Oh, rivers. . . . What did Pascal say about them? "Les rivières sont les chemins qui marchent. . . ." '

This pompous, showing-off way of speaking is not permissible in England. The Englishman is modest and simple. He uses but few words and expresses so much – but so much – with them. An Englishman looking at the same view would remain silent for two or three hours and think about how to put his profound feeling into words. Then he would remark:

'It's pretty, isn't it?'

An English professor of mathematics would say to his maid checking up the shopping list:

'I'm no good at arithmetic, I'm afraid. Please correct me, Jane, if I am wrong, but I believe that the square root of 97344 is 312.'

And about knowledge. An English girl, of course, would be able to learn just a little more about, let us say, geography. But it is just not 'chic' to know whether Budapest is the capital of Roumania, Hungary or Bulgaria. And if she happens to know that Budapest *is* the capital of Roumania, she should at least be perplexed if Bucharest is mentioned suddenly.

It is so much nicer to ask, when someone speaks of Barbados, Banska Bystrica or Fiji:

'Oh those little islands. . . . Are they British?'

(They usually are.)

HOW TO BE RUDE

It is easy to be rude on the Continent. You just shout and call people names of a zoological character.

On a slightly higher level you may invent a few stories against your opponents. In Budapest, for instance, when a rather unpleasant-looking actress joined a nudist club, her younger and prettier colleagues spread the story that she had been accepted only under the condition that she should wear a fig-leaf on her face. Or in the same city there was a painter of limited abilities who was a most successful card-player. A colleague of his remarked once: 'What a spendthrift! All the money he makes on industrious gambling at night, he spends on his painting during the day.'

In England rudeness has quite a different technique. If somebody tells you an obviously untrue story, on the Continent you would remark 'You are a liar, Sir, and a rather dirty one at that.' In England you just say 'Oh, is that so?' Or 'That's rather an unusual story, isn't it?'

When some years ago, knowing ten words of English and using them all wrong, I applied for a translator's job, my would-be employer (or would-be-not-employer) softly remarked: 'I am afraid your English is somewhat unorthodox.' This translated into any continental language would mean: EMPLOYER (to the commissionaire): 'Jean, kick this gentleman down the steps!'

In the last century, when a wicked and unworthy subject annoyed the Sultan of Turkey or the Czar of Russia, he had his head cut of without much ceremony; but when the same happened in England, the monarch declared: 'We are not amused'; and the whole British nation even now, a century later, is immensely proud of how rude their Queen was.

Terribly rude expressions (if pronounced grimly) are: 'I am afraid that . . .' 'unless . . .' 'nevertheless . . .' 'How queer . . .' and 'I am sorry, but . . .'

It is true that quite often you can hear remarks like: 'You'd better see that you get out of here!' Or 'Shut your big mouth!' Or 'Dirty pig!' etc. These remarks are very un-English and are the results of foreign influence. (Dating back, however, to the era of the Danish invasion.)

'Chameau!'

HOW TO COMPROMISE

WISE compromise is one of the basic principles and virtues of the British.

If a continental greengrocer asks 14 schillings (or crowns, or francs, or pengoes, or dinars or leis or δραχμαί or лева, or whatever you like) for a bunch of radishes, and his customer offers 2, and finally they strike a bargain agreeing on 6 schillings, francs, roubles, etc., this is just the low continental habit of bargaining; on the other hand, if the British dockworkers or any workers claim a rise of 4 shillings per day, and the employers first flatly refuse even a penny, but after six weeks strike they agree to a rise of 2 shillings per day – that is yet another proof of the British genius for compromise. Bargaining is a repulsive habit; compromise is one of the highest human virtues – the difference between the two being that the first is practised on the Continent, the latter in Great Britain.

The genius for compromise has another aspect, too. It has a tendency to unite together everything which is bad. English club life, for instance, unites the liabilities of social life with the boredom of solitude. An average English house combines all the curses of civilisation with the vicissitudes of life in the open. It is all right to have windows, but you must not have double windows because double windows would indeed stop the wind from blowing right into the room, and after all, you must be fair and give the wind a chance. It is all right to have central heating in an English home, except the bath room, because that is the only place where you are naked *and* wet at the same time, and you must give British germs a fair chance. The open

A Balkan bargain

fire is an accepted, indeed a traditional, institution.
You sit in front of it and your face is hot whilst your
back is cold. It is a fair compromise between two ex-
tremes and settles the problem of how to burn and
catch cold at the same time. The fact that you may
have a drink at five past six p.m., but that it is a criminal offence to have it at five to six is an extremely wise
compromise between two things (I do not quite know
between what, certainly not between prohibition and
licentiousness), achieving the great aim that nobody
can get drunk between three o'clock and six o'clock in
the afternoon unless he wants to and drinks at home.

English spelling is a compromise between documen-
tary expressions and an elaborate code-system; spending three hours in a queue in front of a cinema is a
compromise between entertainment and asceticism;
the English weather is a fair compromise between rain
and fog; to employ an English charwoman is a compromise between having a dirty house or cleaning it
yourself; Yorkshire pudding is a compromise between
a pudding and the county of Yorkshire.

The Labour Party is a fair compromise between
Socialism and Bureaucracy; the Beveridge Plan is a
fair compromise between being and not being a Socialist at the same time; the Liberal Party is a fair compromise between the Beveridge Plan and Toryism; the
Independent Labour Party is a fair compromise between Independent Labour and a political party; the
Tory-reformers are a fair compromise between revolutionary conservatism and retrograde progress; and the
whole British political life is a huge and non-
compromising fight between compromising Conserva-
tives and compromising Socialists.

HOW TO BE A HYPOCRITE

IF YOU want to be really and truly British, you must become a hypocrite.

Now: how to be a hypocrite?

As some people say that an example explains things better than the best theory, let me try this way.

I had a drink with an English friend of mine in a pub. We were sitting on the high chairs in front of the counter when a flying bomb exploded about a hundred yards away. I was truly and honestly frightened, and when a few seconds later I looked around, I could not see my friend anywhere. At last I noticed that he was lying on the floor, flat as a pancake. When he realized that nothing particular had happened in the pub he got up a little embarrassed, flicked the dust off his suit, and turned to me with a superior and sarcastic smile.

'Good Heavens! Were you so frightened that you couldn't move?'

ABOUT SIMPLE JOYS

IT IS important that you should learn to enjoy simple joys, because that is extremely English. All serious Englishmen play darts and cricket and many other games; a famous English statesman was reported to be catching butterflies in the interval between giving up two European states to the Germans; there was even some misunderstanding with the French because they considered the habit of English soldiers of singing and playing football and hide and seek and blind man's buff slightly childish.

Dull and pompous foreigners are unable to understand why ex-cabinet ministers get together and sing 'Daisy, Daisy' in choir; why serious business men play with toy locomotives while their children learn trigonometry in the adjoining room; why High Court judges collect rare birds when rare birds are rare and they cannot collect many in any case; why it is the ambition of grown-up persons to push a little ball into a small hole; why a great politician who saved England and made history is called a 'jolly good fellow.'

They cannot grasp why people sing when alone and yet sit silent and dumb for hours on end in their clubs, not uttering a word for months in the most distinguished company, and pay twenty guineas a year for the privilege.

Birds of a feather.

THE NATIONAL PASSION

QUEUEING is the national passion of an otherwise dispassionate race. The English are rather shy about it, and deny that they adore it.

On the Continent, if people are waiting at a bus-stop they loiter around in a seemingly vague fashion. When the bus arrives they make a dash for it; most of them leave by the bus and a lucky minority is taken away by an elegant black ambulance car. An Englishman, even if he is alone, forms an orderly queue of one.

The biggest and most attractive advertisements in front of cinemas tell people: Queue here for 4s 6d; Queue here for 9s 3d; Queue here for 16s 8d (inclusive of tax). Those cinemas which do not put out these queueing signs do not do good business at all.

At week-ends an Englishman queues up at the bus-stop, travels out to Richmond, queues up for a boat, then queues up for tea, then queues up for ice cream, then joins a few more odd queues just for the sake of the fun of it, then queues up at the bus-stop and has the time of his life.

Many English families spend lovely evenings at home just by queueing up for a few hours, and the parents are very sad when the children leave them and queue up for going to bed.

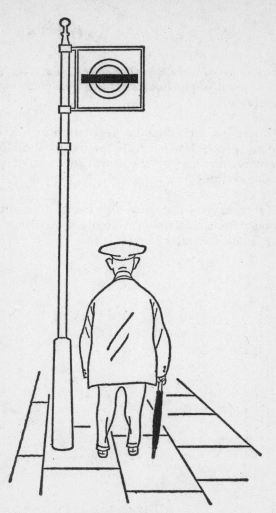

Get thee behind me

H.A.—3

THREE SMALL POINTS

IF YOU go for a walk with a friend, don't say a word for hours; if you go out for a walk with your dog, keep chatting to him.

There is a three-chamber legislation in England. A bill to become law has to be passed by the House of Commons and the House of Lords and finally approved by the Brains Trust.

A fishmonger is the man who mongs fish; the iron-monger and the warmonger do the same with iron and war. They just mong them.

*'And will you be going to Cruft's this year as usual,
Florence?'*

II. How to be a Particular Alien

A BLOOMSBURY INTELLECTUAL

THEY all hate uniforms so much that they all wear a special uniform of their own: brown velvet trousers, canary yellow pullover, green jacket with sky-blue checks.

The suit of clothes has to be chosen with the utmost care and is intended to prove that its wearer does not care for suits and other petty, worldly things.

A walking-stick, too, is often carried by the slightly dandyfied right-wing of the clan.

A golden chain around the ankle, purple velvet shoes and a half-wild angora cat on the shoulders are strongly recommended as they much increase the appearance of arresting casualness.

It is extremely important that the B.I. should *always* wear a three-days beard, as shaving is considered a contemptible bourgeois habit. (The extremist left-wing holds the same view concerning washing, too.) First one will find it a little trying to shave one's four-day beard in such a way that, after shaving, a three days old beard ration should be left on the cheeks, but practise and devoted care will bring their fruits.

A certain amount of rudeness is quite indispensable, because you have to prove day and night that the silly little commonplace rules and customs of society are not meant for *you*. If you find it too difficult to give up these little habits — to say 'Hullo' and 'How d'you do?' and 'Thank you,' etc. — because owing to Auntie

Ars longa, vita brevis

Betty's or Tante Bertha's strict upbringing they have become second nature, then join a Bloomsbury school for bad manners, and after a fortnight you will feel no pang of conscience when stepping deliberately on the corn of the venerable literary editor of a quarterly magazine in the bus.

Literary opinions must be most carefully selected. Statements like this are most impressive. 'There have been altogether two real poets in England: Sir Thomas Wyatt and John Ford. The works of the rest are rubbish.' Of course, you should include, as the third really great, colossal and epoch-making talent your own friend, T. B. Williams, whose neo-expressionist poetry is so terribly deep that the overwhelming majority of editors do not understand it and refuse to publish it. T. B. Williams, you may proudly claim, has never used a comma or a full stop, and what is more, he has improved Apollinaire's and Aragon's primitive technique by the fact that he *does* use question marks. (The generous and extravagant praise of T. B. Williams is absolutely essential, otherwise who will praise *you*?)

As to your own literary activities, your poems, dramas and great novels may lie at the bottom of your drawer in manuscript form. But it is important that you should publish a few literary reviews, scolding and disparaging everything and everybody on earth from a very superior and high-brow point of view, quoting Sir Thomas Wyatt and anything in French and letting the reader feel what *you* would be able to do if you could only find a publisher.

(Some practical advice. It is not difficult to have a few literary reviews published. Many weeklies and monthlies would publish anything in their so-called literary columns, if it costs nothing. You must not call your action unfair competition with qualified

T. B. Williams

reviewers; call it devotion to the 'cause.' Almost every
paper has a cause – if yours has not, invent one, it is
quite easy. And it really does not matter what you
write. I remember one B.I. writing of a significant
philosophical work and admitting in the opening
sentence that he did not understand it; still, I
suppose the review passed as buoyant and alarmingly
sincere.)

Politically you must belong to the extreme left. You
must, however, bear a few things in mind:

1. You must not care a damn about the welfare of
the people in this country or abroad, because that
would be 'practical politics' – and you should only be
interested in the ideological side of matters.

2. Do not belong to any party, because that would
be 'regimentation.' Whatever different parties achieve,
it is much more interesting to criticize everyone than
to belong to the herd.

3. Do not hesitate to scorn Soviet Russia as reactionary and imperialistic, the British Labour Party as a
conglomeration of elderly Trade Union Blimps, the
French Socialists as 'confused people,' the other West-
ern Socialist parties as meek, bourgeois clubs, the
American labour movements as being in the pay of big
business; and call all republicans, communists, anarch-
ists and nihilists 'backward, reactionary crypto-fascists.'

You should also invent a few truly original, construc-
tive theories too, such as:

Only Brahmanism can save the world.

Spiritualism is a factor, growing immensely in
importance, and a practical, working coalition between ghosts and Trotskyites would be highly desir
able.

The abolition of all taxation would enrich the population so enormously that everybody would be able to pay much more taxes than before.

Finally, remember the main point. *Always* be original! It is not as difficult as it sounds: you just have to copy the habits and sayings of a few thousand other B.I.s.

MAYFAIR PLAYBOY

FIX THE little word *de* in front of your name. It has a remarkable attraction. I knew a certain Leo Rosenberg from Graz who called himself Lionel de Rosenberg and was a huge success in Deanery Mews as a Tyrolean nobleman.

Believe that the aim of life is to have a nice time, go to nice places and meet nice people. (Now: to have a nice time means to have two more drinks daily than you can carry; nice places are the halls of great hotels, intimate little clubs, night clubs and private houses with large radiograms and no bookshelves; nice people are those who say silly things in good English – nasty people are those who drop clever remarks as well as their aitches.)

In the old days the man who had no money was not considered a gentleman. In the era of an enlightened Mayfair this attitude has changed. A gentleman may have money or may sponge on his friends; the criterion of a gentleman is that however poor he may be he still refuse to do useful work.

You have to develop your charm with the greatest care. Always laugh at everybody's jokes – but be careful to tell a joke from a serious and profound observation. Be polite in a teasing, nonchalant manner. Sneer at everything you are not intelligent enough to understand. You may flirt with anybody's wife, but respect the ties of illegitimate friendships – unless you have a really good opportunity which it would be such a pity to miss. Don't forget that well-pressed trousers, carefully knotted ties and silk shirts are the greatest of all human values. Never be sober after 6.30 p.m.

Nice versus *nasty*

HOW TO BE A FILM PRODUCER

A LITTLE foreign blood is very advantageous, almost
essential, to become a really great British film producer.

The first aim of a British film producer should be
to teach Hollywood a lesson. Do not be misled, however, by the examples of *Henry V* or *Pygmalion*, which
tend to prove that excellent films can be made of great
plays without changing the out-of-date words of
Shakespeare and the un-film-like dialogues of Shaw by
ten 'experts' who really know better.

Forget these misleading examples because it is
obvious that Shakespeare could not possibly have had
any film technique, and recent research has proved
that he did not even have an eight-seater saloon car
with his own uniformed chauffeur.

You must not touch any typically American subject.
For instance: a young man of Carthage (Kentucky)
who can whistle beautifully goes to town, and after
many disappointments forms his own swing-band and
becomes the leading conductor of New York's night
life – which, if you can take the implication of
Hollywood films seriously, is one of the highest honours
which can be conferred on anyone in that country. At
the same time he falls in love with the cloakroom
attendant of a drug-store* round the corner, a plati-
num-blonde, ravishingly beautiful, who sings a little
better than Galli Curci and Deanna Durbin rolled
into one and, in secret, has the greatest histrionic talent

* Please note my extensive knowledge of the American
language.

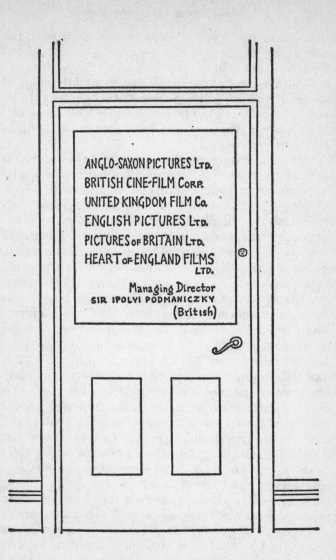

of the century. After a last-minute scandal with the world-famous prima donna she saves the first night of her lover's show in the presence of an audience of six million people by singing Gounod's slightly adapted song. ('If you would be *my* tootsie-bootsie, I would be *your* tootsie-bootsie'.) The young and mighty successful band-leader marries the girl and employs Toscanini to clean his mouth-organ.

Or – to mention just one more example of the serious and 'deep' type of American films – there is a gay, buoyant, happy and miserably poor young man in New Golders Green (Alabama), who becomes tremendously rich just by selling thousands of tractors and jet-propelled aeroplanes to other poor fellows. The richer he becomes, the unhappier he is – which is a subtle point to prove that money does not mean happiness, consequently one had better be content to remain a poor labourer, possibly unemployed. He buys seven huge motor cars and three private planes and is bitter and pained; he builds a magnificent and ostentatious palace and gets gloomier and gloomier; and when the woman he has loved without hope for fifteen years at last falls in love with him, he breaks down completely and groans and moans desperately for three days. To increase the 'deep' meaning of the film they photograph the heroes from the most surprising angles: the cameraman crawls under people's feet, swings on the chandelier, and hides himself in a bowl of soup. Everybody is delighted with the new technique and admires the director's richness of thought.

English film directors follow a different and quite original line. They have discovered somehow that the majority of the public does not consist, after all, of idiots, and that an intelligent film is not necessarily foredoomed to failure. It was a tremendous risk to

*'I understand they then knocked them in the Old Kent
Road'*

make experiments based on this assumption, but it has proved worth while.

There are certain rules you must bear in mind if you want to make a really and truly British film.

1. The 'cockney heart' has definitely been discovered, *i.e.* the fact that even people who drop their aitches have a heart. The discovery was originally made by Mr Noel Coward, who is reported to have met a man who knew someone who had actually seen a cockney from quite near. Ever since it has been essential that a cockney should figure in every British film and display his heart throughout the performance.

2. It has also been discovered that ordinary men occasionally use unparliamentary expressions in the course of their every-day conversation. It has been decided that the more often the adjective referring to the sanguinary character of certain things or persons is used and the exclamation 'Damn!' is uttered, the more realistic and more convincing the film becomes, as able seamen and flight-sergeants sometimes go so far as to say 'Damn!' when they are carried away by passion. All bodies and associations formed to preserve the purity of the English soul should note that I do not agree with this habit – I simply record it. But as it is a habit, the author readily agrees to supply by correspondence a further list of the most expressive military terms which would make any new film surprisingly realistic.

3. Nothing should be good enough for a British film producer. I have heard of a gentleman (I don't know whether the story is true, or only characteristic) who made a film about Egypt and had a sphinx built in the studio. When he and his company sailed to Egypt to make some exterior shots, he took his own sphinx with him to the desert. He was quite right, because first of

all the original sphinx is very old and film people should not use second-hand stuff; secondly, the old sphinx might have been good enough for Egyptians (who are all foreigners, after all) but not for a British film company.

4. As I have seen political events successfully filmed as detective-stories, and historical personages appear as 'great lovers' (and nothing else), I have come to the conclusion that this slight change in the character of a person is highly recommendable, and I advise the filming of *Peter Pan* as a thriller, and the *Concise Oxford Dictionary* as a comic opera.

DRIVING CARS

It is about the same to drive a car in England as anywhere else. To change a punctured tyre in the wind and rain gives about the same pleasure outside London as outside Rio de Janeiro; it is not more fun to try to start up a cold motor with the handle in Moscow than in Manchester, the roughly 50–50 proportion between *driving* an average car and *pushing* it is the same in Sydney and Edinburgh.

There are, however, a few characteristics which distinguish the English motorist from the continental, and some points which the English motorist has to remember.

1. In English towns there is a thirty miles an hour speed-limit and the police keep a watchful eye on law-breakers. The fight against reckless driving is directed extremely skilfully and carefully according to the very best English detective-traditions. It is practically impossible to find out whether you are being followed by a police car or not. There are, however, a few indications which may help people of extraordinary intelligence and with very keen powers of observation:

(a) The police always use a 13 h.p., blue Wolseley car;
(b) three uniformed policemen sit in it; and
(c) on these cars you can read the word POLICE written in large letters in front and rear, all in capitals – lit up during the hours of darkness.

2. I think England is the only country in the world where you have to leave your lights on even if you park

Say not the struggle naught availeth – A. H. Clough

in a brilliantly lit-up street. The advantage being that your battery gets exhausted, you cannot start up again and consequently the number of road accidents are greatly reduced. Safety first!

3. Only motorists can answer this puzzling question: What are taxis for? A simple pedestrian knows that they are certainly not there to carry passengers.

Taxis, in fact, are a Christian institution. They are here to teach drivers modesty and humility. They teach us never to be over-confident; they remind us that we never can tell what the next moment will bring for us, whether we shall be able to drive on or a taxi will bump into us from the back or the side. '. . . and thou shalt fear day and night, and shalt have none assurance of thy life' (Deut., chapter 28, verse 66).

4. There is a huge ideological warfare going on behind the scenes of the motorist world.

Whenever you stop your car in the City, the West End or many other places, two or three policemen rush at you and tell you that you must not park *there*. Where may you park? They shrug their shoulders. There are a couple of spots on the South Coast and in a village called Minchinhampton. Three cars may park there for half an hour every other Sunday morning between 7 and 8 a.m.

The police are perfectly right. After all, cars have been built to run, and run fast, so they should not stop.

This healthy philosophy of the police has been seriously challenged by a certain group of motorists who maintain that cars have been built to park and not to move. These people drive out to Hampstead Heath or Richmond on beautiful, sunny days, pull up all their windows and go to sleep. They do not get a spot of air; they are miserably uncomfortable; they have nightmares, and the whole procedure is called 'spending a lovely afternoon in the open.'

THREE GAMES FOR BUS DRIVERS

IF YOU become a bus driver there are three lovely and very popular games you must learn to play.

1. *Blind man's buff*. When you turn right just signal by showing two millimetres of your finger-tips. It is great fun when motorists do not notice your signal and run into your huge bus with their tiny cars.

2. *Hide and seek*. Whenever you approach a request stop hide behind a large lorry or another bus and when you have almost reached the stop shoot off at a terrific speed. It is very amusing to see people shake their fists at you. It is ten to one they miss some important business appointment.

3. *Hospital game*. If you have to stop for one reason or another, never wait until the conductor rings the bell. If you start moving quickly and unexpectedly, and if you are lucky – and in slippery weather you have a very good chance – people will fall on top of one another. This looks extremely funny from the driver's seat. (Sometimes the people themselves, who fall into a muddy pool and break their legs, make a fuss, but, alas! every society has its bores who have no sense of humour and cannot enjoy a joke at their own expense.)

You can't catch me!

HOW TO PLAN A TOWN

BRITAIN, far from being a 'decadent democracy', is a Spartan country. This is mainly due to the British way of building towns, which dispenses with the reasonable comfort enjoyed by all the other weak and effeminate peoples of the world.

Medieval warriors wore steel breast-plates and leggings not only for defence but also to keep up their fighting spirit; priests of the Middle Ages tortured their bodies with hair-shirts; Indian yogis take their daily nap lying on a carpet of nails to remain fit. The English plan their towns in such a way that these replace the discomfort of steel breast-plates, hair-shirts and nail-carpets.

On the Continent doctors, lawyers, booksellers — just to mention a few examples — are sprinkled all over the city, so you can call on a good or at least expensive doctor in any district. In England the idea is that it is the address that makes the man. Doctors in London are crowded in Harley Street, solicitors in Lincoln's Inn Fields, second-hand-bookshops in Charing Cross Road, newspaper offices in Fleet Street, tailors in Saville Row, car-merchants in Great Portland Street, theatres around Piccadilly Circus, cinemas in Leicester Square, etc. If you have a chance of replanning London you can greatly improve on this idea. All greengrocers should be placed in Hornsey Lane (N6), all butchers in Mile End (E1), and all gentlemen's conveniences in Bloomsbury (WC).

Now I should like to give you a little practical advice on how to build an English town.

Mortification of the flesh

You must understand that an English town is a vast conspiracy to mislead foreigners. You have to use century-old little practices and tricks.

1. First of all, never build a street straight. The English love privacy and do not want to see one end of the street from the other end. Make sudden curves in the streets and build them S-shaped too; the letters L, T, V, Y, W and O are also becoming increasingly popular. It would be a fine tribute to the Greeks to build a few Φ and Θ-shaped streets; it would be an ingenious compliment to the Russians to favour the shape Я, and I am sure the Chinese would be more than flattered to see some 雝-shaped thoroughfares.

2. Never build the houses of the same street in a straight line. The British have always been a freedom-loving race and the 'freedom to build a muddle' is one of their most ancient civic rights.

3. Now there are further camouflage possibilities in the numbering of houses. Primitive continental races put even numbers on one side, odd numbers on the other, and you always know that small numbers start from the north or west. In England you have this system, too; but you may start numbering your houses at one end, go up to a certain number on the same side, then continue on the other side, going back in the opposite direction.

You may leave out some numbers if you are superstitious; and you may continue the numbering in a side street; you may also give the same number to two or three houses.

But this is far from the end. Many people refuse to have numbers altogether, and they choose names. It is very pleasant, for instance, to find a street with three hundred and fifty totally similar bungalows and look for 'The Bungalow'. Or to arrive in a street where all the houses have a charming view of a hill and try to find 'Hill View'. Or search for 'Seven Oaks' and find a house with three apple-trees.

4. Give a different name to the street whenever it bends; but if the curve is so sharp that it really makes two different streets, you may keep the same name. On the other hand, if, owing to neglect, a street has been built in a straight line it must be called by many different names (High Holborn, New Oxford Street, Oxford Street, Bayswater Road, Notting Hill Gate, Holland Park and so on).

5. As some cute foreigners would be able to learn their way about even under such circumstances, some further precautions are necessary. Call streets by various names: street, road, place, mews, crescent, avenue, rise, lane, way, grove, park, gardens, alley, arch, path, walk, broadway, promenade, gate, terrace, vale, view, hill, etc.*

Now two further possibilities arise:

(*a*) Gather all sorts of streets and squares of the same name in one neighbourhood: Belsize Park, Belsize

* While this book was at the printers a correspondence in *The Times* showed that the English have almost sixty synonyms for 'street.' If you add to these the street names which stand alone (Piccadilly, Strand, etc.) and the accepted and frequently used double names ('Garden Terrace', 'Church Street', 'Park Road', etc.) the number of street names reaches or exceeds a hundred. It has been suggested by one correspondent that this clearly proves what wonderful imagination the English have. I believe it proves the contrary. A West End street in London is not called 'Haymarket' because the playful fancy of Londoners populates the district with romantically clad medieval food dealers, but simply because they have not noticed as yet that the hay trade has considerably declined between Piccadilly and Pall Mall in the last three hundred years.

Street, Belsize Road, Belsize Gardens, Belsize Green, Belsize Circus, Belsize Yard, Belsize Viaduct, Belsize Arcade, Belsize Heath, etc.

(*b*) Place a number of streets of *exactly* the same name in different districts. If you have about twenty Princes Squares and Warwick Avenues in the town, the muddle – you may claim without immodesty – will be complete.

6. Street names should be painted clearly and distinctly on large boards. Then hide these boards carefully. Place them too high or too low, in shadow and darkness, upside down and inside out, or, even better, lock them up in a safe in your bank, otherwise they may give people some indication about the names of the streets.

7. In order to break down the foreigner's last vestige of resistance and shatter his morale, one further trick is advisable: Introduce the system of squares – real squares, I mean – which run into four streets like this:

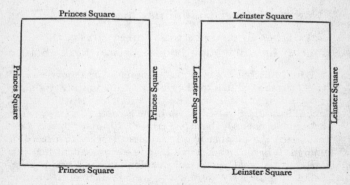

With this simple device it is possible to build a street of which the two sides have different names.

P.S. – I have been told that my above-described theory

is all wrong and is only due to my Central European conceit, because the English do not care for the opinion of foreigners. In every other country, it has been explained, people just build streets and towns following their own common sense. England is the only country of the world where there is a Ministry of Town and Country Planning. That is the real reason for the muddle.

CIVIL SERVANT

THERE is a world of difference between the English Civil Servant and the continental.

On the Continent (not speaking now of the Scandinavian countries), Civil Servants assume a certain military air. They consider themselves little generals; they use delaying tactics; they cannot withdraw armies, so they withdraw permissions; they thunder like cannons and their speech is like machine-gun fire; they cannot lose battles, they lose documents instead. They consider that the sole aim of human society is to give jobs to Civil Servants. A few wicked individuals, however (contemptible little groups of people who are not Civil Servants), conspire against them, come to them with various requests, complaints, problems, etc., with the sole purpose of making a nuisance of themselves. These people get the reception they deserve. They are kept waiting in cold and dirty ante-chambers (some of them clean these rooms occasionally, but they are hired commissionaires whose duty it is to re-dirty these rooms every morning); they have to stand, often at attention, whilst they are spoken to; they are always shouted at in a rude manner and their requests are turned down with malicious pleasure. Sometimes – this is a popular cat and mouse game – they are sent to another office on the fifth floor, from there they are directed to a third office in the basement, where they are told that they should not have come there at all and sent back to the original office. In that office they are thoroughly told off in acrimonious language and dispatched to the fifth floor once again, from there to the basement and the procedure goes on endlessly until the poor fellows

'*Alors, ECOUTEZ madame —*'

either get tired of the whole business and give up in despair or become raving lunatics and go to an asylum asking for admittance. If the latter case occurs they are told in the reception office that they have come to the wrong place, they should go to another office on the fifth floor, from which they are sent down to the basement, etc., etc., until they give up being lunatics.

(If you want to catch me out and ask me who are then the people who fill the continental lunatic asylums, I can give you the explanation: they are all Civil Servants who know the ways and means of dealing with officials and succeed in getting in somehow.)

If a former continental Civil Servant thought that this martial behaviour would be accepted by the British public he would be badly mistaken. The English Civil Servant considers himself no soldier but a glorified businessman. He is smooth and courteous; he smiles in a superior way; he is agreeable and obliging.

If so – you may ask – how can he achieve the supreme object of his vast and noble organization, namely, not to transact any business and be left in peace to read a good murder story undisturbed?

There are various, centuries-old, true British traditions to secure this aim.

1. All orders and directives to the public are worded in such a way that they should have no meaning whatever.

2. All official letters are written in such a language that the oracles of Delphi sound as examples of clear, outspoken, straightforward statements compared with them.

3. Civil Servants never make decisions, they only promise to 'consider,' – 'consider favourably' – or – and this is the utmost – 'reconsider' certain questions.

4. In principle the British Civil Servant stands always at the disposal of the public. In practice he is either in 'conference' or out for lunch, or in but having his tea, or just out. Some develop an admirable technique of going out for tea before coming back from lunch.

The British Civil Servant, unlike the rough bully we often find on the Continent, is the Obedient Servant of the public. Before the war, an alien in this country was ordered to leave. He asked for extension of his staying permit, but was refused. He stayed on all the same, and after a while he received the following letter (I quote from memory):

Dear Sir,
The Under-Secretary of State presents his compliments and regrets that he is unable to reconsider your case, and begs to inform you that unless you kindly leave this country within 24 hours you will be forcibly expelled.

Your Obedient Servant,
x x x

On the Continent rich and influential people, or those who have friends, cousins, brothers-in-law, tenants, business associates, etc., in an office may have their requests fulfilled. In England there is no such corruption and your obedient servant just will not do a thing whoever you may be. And this is the real beauty of democracy.

JOURNALISM OR THE FREEDOM OF THE PRESS

The Fact

THERE was some trouble with the Buburuk tribe in the Pacific Island, Charamak. A party of ten English and two American soldiers, under the command of Capt. R. L. A. T. W. Tilbury, raided the island and took 217 revolutionary, native troublemakers prisoner and wrecked two large oil-dumps. The party remained ashore an hour-and-a-half and returned to their base without loss to themselves.

How to report this event? It depends which newspaper you work for.

THE TIMES

... It would be exceedingly perilous to overestimate the significance of the raid, but it can be fairly proclaimed that it would be even more dangerous to underestimate it. The success of the raid clearly proves that the native defences are not invulnerable; it would be fallacious and deceptive, however, to conclude that these defences are vulnerable. The number of revolutionaries captured cannot be safely stated, but it seems likely that the number is well over 216 but well under 218.

IN THE HOUSE

You may become an M.P. (Nothing is impossible – this would not be even unprecedented.) You may hear then the following statement by a member of Her Majesty's Government:

'Concerning the two wrecked oil-dumps I can give

this information to the House. In the first half of this year the amount of native oil destroyed by the Army, Navy and the R.A.F. – excluding however, the Fleet Air Arm – is one-half as much as three times the amount destroyed during the corresponding months of the previous year, seven and a half times as much as the two-fifths destroyed two years ago and three-quarters as much again as twelve times one-sixth destroyed three years ago.' (Loud cheers from the Government benches.)

You jump to your feet and ask this question:

YOU: Is the Right Hon. Gentleman aware that people in this country are puzzled and worried by the fact that Charamak was raided and not Ragamak?

THE RIGHT HON. MEMBER: I have nothing to add to my statement given on 2nd August, 1892.

EVENING STANDARD

(*Londoner's Diary*)

The most interesting feature of the Charamak raid is the fact that Reggie Tilbury is the fifth son of the Earl of Bayswater. He was an Oxford Blue, a first-class cricketer and quite good at polo. When I talked to his wife (Lady Clarisse, the daughter of Lord Elasson) at Claridges today, she wore a black suit and a tiny black hat with a yellow feather in it. She said: 'Reggie was always very much interested in warfare.' Later she re-marked: 'It was clever of him, wasn't it?'

You may write a letter to the Editor of *The Times*:

Sir, – In connection with the Charamak raid I should like to mention as a matter of considerable interest that it was in that little Pacific Island that the distinguished English poet, John Flat, wrote his famous poem 'The Cod' in 1693. Yours, etc. ...

An early interest in warfare

You may read this answer on the following day.

Sir, – I am very grateful to Mr . . . for calling attention to John Flat's poem 'The Cod.' May I be allowed to use this opportunity, however, to correct a widespread and in my view very unfortunate error which the great masses of the British people seem to share with your correspondent. 'The Cod,' although John Flat started writing it in 1693, was only finished in the early days of January 1694.

Yours, etc. . . .

If you are the London correspondent of the American paper

THE OKLAHOMA SUN

simply cable this:

'Yanks Conquer Pacific Ocean.'

IF NATURALIZED

THE VERB *to naturalize* clearly proves what the British think of you. Before you are admitted to British citizenship you are not even considered a natural human being. I looked up the word natural (na'tural) in the Pocket Oxford Dictionary (p. 251); it says: *Of or according to or provided by nature, physically existing, innate, instinctive, normal, not miraculous or spiritual or artificial or conventional.* . . . Note that before you obtain British citizenship, they simply doubt that you are provided by nature.

According to the Pocket Oxford Dictionary the word 'natural' has a second meaning, too: *Half-witted person.* This second meaning, however, is irrelevant from the point of view of our present argument.

If you are tired of not being provided by nature, not being physically existing and being miraculous and

conventional at the same time, apply for British citizenship. Roughly speaking, there are two possibilities: it will be granted to you, or not.

In the first case you must recognize and revise your attitude to life. You must pretend that you are everything you are not and you must look down upon everything you are.

Copy the attitude of an English acquaintance of mine – let us call him Gregory Baker. He, an English solicitor, feels particularly deep contempt for the following classes of people: foreigners, Americans, Frenchmen, Irishmen, Scotsmen and Welshmen, Jews, workers, clerks, poor people, non-professional men, business men, actors, journalists and literary men, women, solicitors who do not practise in his immediate neighbourhood, solicitors who are hard up and solicitors who are too rich, Socialists, Liberals, Tory-reformers (Communists are not worthy even of his contempt); he looks down upon his mother, because she has a business mind, his wife, because she comes from a non-professional county family, his brother, because although he is a professional officer he does not serve with the Guards, Hussars, or at least with a county regiment. He adores and admires his seven-years old son, because the shape of his nose resembles his own.

If naturalized, remember these rules:

1. You must start eating porridge for breakfast and allege that you like it.

2. Speak English with your former compatriots. Deny that you know any foreign language (including your mother tongue). The knowledge of foreign languages is very un-English. A little French is permissible, but only with an atrocious accent.

3. Revise your library. Get rid of all foreign writers

whether in the original or translated into English. The works of Dostoyevsky should be replaced by a volume on English Birds; the collected works of Proust by a book called 'Interior Decoration in the Regency Period'; and Pascal's *Pensées* by the 'Life and Thoughts of a Scottish Salmon'.

4. Speaking of your new compatriots, always use the first person plural.

In this aspect, though, a certain caution is advisable. I know a na'turalized Britisher who, talking to a young man, repeatedly used the phrase 'We Englishmen.' The young man looked at him, took his pipe out of his mouth and remarked softly: 'Sorry, Sir, I'm a Welshman,' turned his back on him and walked away.

The same gentleman was listening to a conversation. It was mentioned that the Japanese had claimed to have shot down 22 planes.

'What – ours?' he asked indignantly.

His English hostess answered icily:

'No – *ours*.'

MORE ABOUT PENGUINS
AND PELICANS

For further information about books available from
Penguins please write to Dept EP, Penguin Books Ltd,
Harmondsworth, Middlesex UB7 ODA.

In the U.S.A.: For a complete list of books available
from Penguins in the United States write to Dept CS,
Penguin Books, 625 Madison Avenue, New York, New
York 10022.

In Canada: For a complete list of books available from
Penguins in Canada write to Penguin Books Canada Ltd,
2801 John Street, Markham, Ontario L3R 1B4.

In Australia: For a complete list of books available from
Penguins in Australia write to the Marketing Depart-
ment, Penguin Books Australia Ltd, P.O. Box 257,
Ringwood, Victoria 3134.

George Mikes in Penguins

THE LAND OF THE RISING YEN

Everyone writes about the tea ceremony in Japan, but who, except George Mikes, notices the way the rubbish is thrown out? Everyone reports his own reaction to the Japanese sense of tradition: but who else spots the reaction of the Japanese to their own sense of tradition?

Whether he is describing morals or manners, George Mikes looks at the Japanese as he looks at the rest of mankind: with his own inscrutable blend of curiosity, respect, affection and charm.

Look out for these in Penguins!

TALES FROM THE LITTLE WORLD OF DON CAMILLO
Giovanni Guareschi

Gloriously comic and vibrant with sly chuckles, Don Camillo's Little World has captured the hearts and minds of generations.

Here, in the Po Valley, the Good Lord strives to keep the peace between the honest hot-tempered village priest and his deadly opponent, Peppone, the Communist mayor. Cheering – and criticizing – from the sidelines, He ensures that the Cold War does not get too chilly.

RUMPOLE'S RETURN
John Mortimer

Has Rumpole *really* hung up his wig and deserted the Courts of British Justice?

He is supposed by all and sundry to be enjoying his well-earned retirement basking soggily in the Florida sun beside his cherished helpmeet (She Who Must Be Obeyed), replete with healthy orange juice and airmail copies of *The Times*, learning to rap with strangers.

But Rumpole is made of sterner stuff, and the merest whiff of a meaty Blood case and of his sworn enemy, Judge Bullingham, sets the venerable war-horse a-twitching. And, courtesy of Gaelic Airlines (Budget Airlines Standby), Rumpole descends on the dear old Chambers to take command once again.

also by John Mortimer

Rumpole of the Bailey
The Trials of Rumpole

Recent fiction from Penguins

MY UNCLE OSWALD
Roald Dahl

The long-awaited novel in which Uncle Oswald discovers the electrifying properties of the Sudanese Blister Beetle and the gorgeous Yasmin Howcomely – a girl absolutely soaked in sex – and arranges the seduction of all the great men of his time for his own wicked, irreverent reasons.

'Deliciously silly' – *Observer*
'Rollicking, raunchy, OUTRAGEOUS' – *Evening Standard*

SCHULTZ
J. P. Donleavy

Schultz, Sigmund Franz, impresario producer of flops in London's West End. He's a walking or sometimes chauffeur-driven and often boot-propelled disaster area. Which disasters are often indulgently plotted by his aristocratic partners His Amazing Grace Basil Nectarine and the languid Binky. But more frequently caused by Schultz's desperate need to seduce as many beautiful women as is humanly possible – and then more.

THE 400
Stephen Sheppard

'Looking at the Bank of England that night, George had become quiet and calm. His American voice spoke softly – "We'll take her," he said.'

So begins an adventure so daring, a scheme so breathtakingly elegant, a fraud so cheekily flamboyant that it defies the imagination . . . Stephen Sheppard's international bestseller, set in 1872 in London, Rio de Janeiro and Europe, is as full of verve and dash as his characters – four rascals you'll never forget.

'Could rival Forsyth' – *Now!*
'Blockbusting' – *Sunday Express*

Recently published in Penguins

CLEMENTINE CHURCHILL
Mary Soames

Lady Soames describes her book as 'a labour of love – but I trust not of blind love', others have acclaimed it as one of the outstanding biographies of the decade:

'Perceptive and affectionate, shrewd and tender ... a joy to read' – Elizabeth Longford

'Lady Soames has carried out the extremely delicate and difficult task of writing the real story of her mother. I found it particularly moving because I had a very deep affection for her father and mother' – Harold Macmillan

'A triumph ... her subject, unknown yet well-known, is enthralling' – Eric James in *The Times*

A PORTRAIT OF JANE AUSTEN
David Cecil

David Cecil's magnificent and highly enjoyable portrait of a writer who represents for us, as no other, the elegance, grace and wit of Georgian England.

'A masterpiece which ought to be in every educated home. Nobody could have done it better, nobody will be able to do it so well again. The book is a monument to subject and author' – Auberon Waugh in *Books and Bookmen*

THE SEVENTIES
Christopher Booker

From the rise of Mrs Thatcher to the murder of Lord Mountbatten, from the energy crisis to the trial of Jeremy Thorpe, from the Cult of Nostalgia to the Collapse of the Modern Movement in the Arts ... In this series of penetrating essays Christopher Booker explores the underlying themes which shaped our thoughts and our lives in the 'seventies.

'Booker is quite compulsive' – *Punch*
'Constantly stimulating...savagely funny' – *Evening Standard*

ROOM AT THE TOP
John Braine

Joe Lampton wants to get out of the seedy pen-pushing offices of the Town Hall into the big bright world beyond – fast cars, women, a gold signet ring – everything that comes with success. To enter this world Joe knew that he would have to make sacrifices. What he didn't know was that he would have to betray love and destroy friendships – nor did he realize just how much he would care. An original 'angry young man' of the 'fifties, Joe Lampton has become the northern small-town hero of our time.

CHANGING PLACES
David Lodge

The plate-glass, concrete jungle of Euphoria State University, U.S.A., and the damp red-brick University of Rummidge have an annual exchange scheme. Normally the exchange passes without comment. But when Philip Swallow swaps with Professor Zapp the fates play their hand, and the two academics find themselves enmeshed in a spiralling involvement on opposite sides of the Atlantic. Nobody is immune: students, colleagues, even wives are swapped as the tension increases.

'Three star rating for a laugh a line' – Auberon Waugh

HURRY ON DOWN
John Wain

Fresh from University, a dismal three-week stay in Stotwell (to concentrate his mind), a brush with his future in-laws, and thoughts of his family (like a vanilla blancmange), Charles Lumley decides to escape. The question is unnervingly simple: what is he going to do with the rest of *his* life?

The forerunner of *Lucky Jim* and *Room at the Top*, John Wain's glorious first novel, published in 1953, has since become a classic.

'Very funny ... fresh, unhackneyed and excellently observed' – *Listener*

Kingsley Amis

JAKE'S THING

'The funniest thing he has done since *Lucky Jim*' – *Daily Mail*

In his hilarious, *outrageous* and wickedly funny story of Jake and his lost libido, Kingsley Amis does not pull any punches, but takes some well-aimed, unerring swipes at the crankier fringes of psychotherapy and at sex – seventies-style.

'Makes you sick laughing . . . all good, unfair, vicious stuff' – *Sunday Telegraph*

'I enjoyed it tremendously' – Auberon Waugh

'Very funny' – *Daily Telegraph*

'Vintage Amis . . . he has probably given as much pleasure as any novelist of his generation' – *Scotsman*

GIRL, 20

'Sir Roy Vandervane, elderly English composer-conductor . . . combines the roles of eternal lecher and incurable progressive. His foil and mistress is the appalling seventeen-year-old Sylvia, representing in her repulsive person all that is least attractive in contemporary youth . . . not only a very funny book, it also hits dozens of nails smartly on the head' – *Observer*

'Kingsley Amis has a wicked ear for such things as imbec-ilities of matrimonial conversation and a stiletto pen for pseuds' – *The Times*

Also published

The Anti-Death League
My Enemy's Enemy
Lucky Jim
One Fat Englishman
Take a Girl Like You

Forthcoming

Russian Hide-and-Seek

Spike Milligan

THE Q ANNUAL

If you've seen Spike Miliigan's Q Series on television you'll enjoy this book, if you haven't – you'd better begin here.

In glorious black and white Spike sings his evening dress to sleep; measures Napoleon for half a coffin; impersonates John Hanson in 'On the Buses'; speaks out on behalf of oppressed minorities from the Royal Family to the Lone Ranger. There is a rare photograph of Ivan's wife Mrs Ethel Terrible, and dramatic new evidence on the liquefaction of Harry Secombe, Princess Anne's birthday, the electric banana . . .

OPEN HEART UNIVERSITY

Following the bestselling *Small Dreams of a Scorpion* comes this second collection of the poems of Spike Milligan.
'Somewhere inside the Goon, a small-sized William Blake is always struggling to get out and make himself heard' – *Punch*
'Compassionate, perceptive, outraged and tender' – *Evening News*

and

Adolf Hitler : My Part in His Downfall
'Rommel?' 'Gunner Who?'
Monty – His Part in My Victory
Mussolini – His Part in My Downfall
Puckoon
Small Dreams of a Scorpion
Transports of Delight
The Spike Milligan Letters (Edited by Norma Farnes)
William McGonagall : The Truth at Last (with Jack Hobbs)